Thomas Goode Jones

Last days of the Army of Northern Virginia

Thomas Goode Jones

Last days of the Army of Northern Virginia

ISBN/EAN: 9783337113018

Printed in Europe, USA, Canada, Australia, Japan

Cover: Foto ©Andreas Hilbeck / pixelio.de

More available books at **www.hansebooks.com**

Last Days of the **Army** of Northern Virginia

AN ADDRESS

DELIVERED BY

GOV. THOS. G. JONES,

BEFORE

THE VIRGINIA DIVISION OF THE ASSOCIATION OF

THE ARMY OF NORTHERN VIRGINIA

AT

THE ANNUAL MEETING,

RICHMOND, VA., OCTOBER 12TH, 1893.

[RESOLUTION.]

Headquarters Virginia Division of the

ASSOCIATION OF THE ARMY OF NORTHERN VIRGINIA.

RICHMOND, VA., October 12th, 1893.

At the regular annual meeting of the Virginia Division of the Association of the Army of Northern Virginia, held this day in the State Capitol, the following proceedings were had:

Col. Richard L. Maury offered the following resolution:

"*Resolved*, That the thanks of this Association be tendered Governor Thomas G. Jones, of Alabama, for his able address on "The Last Days of the Army of Northern Virginia," and that a copy of same be requested for publication and the archives of the Association."

Which was unanimously adopted.

Test,   THOMAS ELLETT,
                                                          Secretary.

[REPLY.]

MONTGOMERY, ALA., November 7th, 1893.

CAPT. THOMAS ELLETT,
          Secretary, Virginia Division,
                    Association of Army of Northern Virginia,
                              Richmond, Va.:

DEAR SIR—In compliance with the resolution enclosed in your letter of the 30th ult., I take pleasure in sending herewith copy of the address. I have delayed doing so until to-day, to perfect some of the notes to the text.

Thanking the Association for the many kindnesses shown me, I am,

          Yours most truly,

                              THOS. G. JONES.

Last Days of the Army of Northern Virginia

AN ADDRESS

DELIVERED BY

GOV. THOS. G. JONES,

BEFORE

THE VIRGINIA DIVISION OF THE ASSOCIATION OF
THE ARMY OF NORTHERN VIRGINIA

AT

THE ANNUAL MEETING,

RICHMOND, VA., OCTOBER 12TH, 1893.

Gov. Jones, after appropriately acknowledging the kind introduction of the Chairman, said:

Posterity will admit, as Greeley does in his "American Conflict" that the Confederacy had no alternative to staying its arm at Sumter, but "its own dissolution." The smoke in Charleston harbor had hardly cleared away before there arose in sight of the world the heroic figure of the Army of Northern Virginia. Many have questioned its cause, but none have ever doubted it.

Washington and Richmond are about 120 miles apart; and in assault or defense of these cities each section put forth its mightiest effort. The first army marched out from Washington for Richmond in 1861, and the Army of Northern Virginia routed it at Manassas.

In 1862 it repelled the mighty army of invasion which came in sight of the spires of Richmond—defeated it and another army a second time on the plains of Manassas—baffled or beat other armies at Winchester, Cross-Keys, and Port Republic—advancing northward captured Harpers Ferry with 11,000 prisoners, fought a drawn battle in Maryland—and hurled back a mighty foe at Fredericksburg.

£470
J. T.

In 1863, it defeated "the finest army on the planet" at Chancellorsville, and leaping Northward carried its standard into Pennsylvania, where it failed to drive the foe from the heights of Gettysburg, and then returning to its own soil again threw the hostile army back on Washington, and yet again balked invasion at Mine-Run. During that year it allowed no invading army to approach at any time within five days march of its capital.

In 1864 it hurled back one column at Bermuda Hundreds, another at New Market, still another at Lynchburg—won victory at Kernstown and Monocacy, and assailed the outer walls of Washington. With the main invading army, under its sturdiest leader, it sought and nearly succeeded in a death grapple in the Wilderness—repeatedly repulsed it with frightful loss at Spottsylvania—won another Fredericksburg at Coal-Harbor—repelled with awful slaughter all attacks in front of Petersburg; and for ten long months defended two cities 22 miles apart, until the thin line worn by attrition and starvation, was broken through at last.

Four awful years passed before the armies which started from Washington trod the streets of Richmond; and in each of those years the Army of Northern Virginia startled Washington with the roll of its drum, or fought battles for its possession north of the Potomac.

The last hours of such an army have not received that consideration from the historian which they deserve. Knowing it will prove of interest to the survivors of that glorious army, and that perchance something I may say may serve to direct abler minds and pens to this rich epoch in its history, I venture to address my comrades to-night on "The last days of the Army of Northern Virginia."

It is impossible, of course, in the scope or compass of such a paper, to give in detail the history of the events which forced the evacuation of Richmond, or to describe, except in the simplest way, the movements of the army from Petersburg to Appomattox. I shall not be able even to mention all the actions on the retreat or to describe many of its noted scenes or to recall many heroic feats of arms, or to attempt, were I worthy to pronounce it, any eulogy upon its great commander.

THE STRENGTH OF THE CONTENDING ARMIES.

The odds against which the army contended, both moral and physical, are not comprehended even now by many who took part in the struggle. It is material, therefore, to consider the strength and conditions of the two armies at the commencement of the operations which ended at Appomattox.

The exact strength of the contending armies at the opening of hostilities, March 25th, 1865, is a matter of some dispute. The morning reports and field returns of the two armies, however, give data from which the strength of each can be determined with substantial accuracy.

Major General Humphreys, at one time Chief of Staff to Gen'l Meade, and afterwards a corps commander in his army, a writer of great ability and fairness, states that the total effective of Lee's army, on the 25th day of March, 1865, was infantry 46,000, field artillery 5,000, and cavalry 6,000, making a total of not less than 57,000 officers and men. He appears to reach these figures on the assumption that Wise's Brigade, 2,000 strong, was not included in the reports of Anderson's corps, and that Rosser's cavalry was also omitted from the last morning returns of the Department of Northern Virginia of February 20th, 1865. Not having the returns before me for inspection, it is impossible to determine whether the assumption is well founded.*

The last morning report of the Department of Northern Virginia was made February 20, 1865, and included not only the troops around Petersburg and Richmond, but those in the Valley and guarding bridges and railroads in the Department, and other unattached commands, and gives a total present for duty, in the entire Department, of 59,093 men. 5,169 of the number thus reported were stationed either in the Valley or on the railroad defences, leaving the total present of 53,924, on the Richmond and Petersburg lines on February 20, 1865. To this should be added the command of General Ewell, who had about 2,760 infantry in the Department of Richmond, under General Custis Lee, and the Naval Batallion under Commodore Tucker. Includ-

*Col. Taylor, in "Four years with General Lee," speaks of the morning return of February 28th, 1865, while Humphreys and other Northern writers speak of the return of February 20th, 1865, as being the "last morning report of the A. N. V. on file in the War Department." All evidently refer to the same report since the figures in each are the same.

ing these in the total of the troops immediately around Richmond and Petersburg, General Lee's present for duty on the 20th of February, 1865, would amount to 57,000, in round numbers, of all branches of the service. If we deduct from this number the 6,041 cavalry and 5,392 artillery, it would give Lee six weeks before the final operations began, 45,567 muskets for the defense of his entire line of 37 miles from right to left. Of the cavalry present 2,500 were dismounted for lack of horses, and the horses of the remainder were hardly fit for use owing to the arduous service, the effects of the hard winter, and the scarcity of forage.

Between the 20th February and the 1st of April, 1865, owing to the gloomy outlook of the cause, and the great suffering of the men and their families at home, the desertions from Lee's army, according to the statement of his Adjutant General, amounted to about 3,000. In the attack on Hare's Hill, on March 25th, the Confederate loss in killed, wounded and missing was about 3,500, to which should be added the loss on other parts of the line of about one thousand men, so that on the morning of the 29th of March, when Grant commenced his final movement, and every available infantry man was in line, Lee could muster a little over 38,000 muskets to withstand the attack.* This estimate is substantially that of Swinton, another very careful Northern writer, who states that at this time, "from his left north east of Richmond, to his right beyond Peterstersburg as far as Hather's Run, there were 35 miles of breastworks which it behooved Lee to guard, and all the force remaining to him "was 37,000 muskets and a small body of broken down horse."

Mr. Stanton, Federal Secretary of War, reported that Gen'l Grant had available on the 1st of March, 1865, in the armies of Meade, Ord and Sheridan, an available total of all arms of 162,-

---

*My estimate of the number of muskets available to Lee at the commencement of final operations, after deducting the losses by desertion between that time and Feb'y. 20th, 1865, and the casualties of March 25th, is a little less than Col. Taylor gives him a month earlier before these casualties occurred. He says "it will be seen on Feby. 28th 1865, Gen'l. Lee had available 39,879 muskets." I reach my estimate by including the number of troops under Custis Lee and the Naval batallion, which are not borne on the last morning report of the N. N. V. of Feby. 20th, 1865, and accept, though it may be erroneously, the conclusion of Humphrey's that Wise's brigade is not included in these returns. Col. Taylor may be right and my estimate may be erroneous. My purpose in accepting the figures of Humphreys, is to show the disparity of numbers, even conceding all reputable claims of our strength by writers on the other side.

239. General Humphreys, argues that this report does not correctly state the "available force present for duty," because it includes not only the "officers and enlisted men of every branch of the service present for duty, but all those on extra or detail duty, as well as in arrest or confinement." He claims that the available strength of the army of the Potomac on the 1st of March 1865, by this method of return, is increased by 16,000, or an addition of about one-eighth to its real fighting strength. Making this deduction from the total effective of 162.239 reported by the Secretary of War and based on the returns from those armies, we would have a total of Grant's effective men, according to Gen'l Humphrey's method of computation, of 146.239.* Gen'l Humphreys taking the morning reports of March 31st, 1865. of men "present for duty, equipped" (which he states is meant to represent the effective force, or total number of men available for line of battle, and excluding all non-combatants, sick, etc..) gives the effective fighting strength of the army of the Potomac at 69,000 infantry, and 6.000 field artillery; that of the army of the James at 32,000 infantry, 3,0-0 field artillery, and 1,700 cavalry under McKenzie, and Sheridan's enlisted men, exclusive of officers, of the cavalry, at 13,000—a total in round numbers of 124,700 men, according to Gen'l. Humphreys.

Badeau, "Military History of Ulysses S. Grant," Vol. 3, p. 438, states:

"On the 25th of March. 1865, Lee had still seventy thousand effective men in the lines at Richmond and Petersburg, while the armies of the Potomac and the James and Sheridan's cavalry. constituting Grant's immediate command, numbered one hundred and eleven thousand soldiers."

In an elaborate note on p. 439, he assails Col. Taylor's statement in "Four Years with General Lee," that Lee had at that time only 39,879 available muskets for the defence of the Richmond and Petersburg lines, and endeavors to support his (Badeau's) statement of Lee's effective strength by a remarkably vulnerable argument.

Badeau writes as if he thought Lee's return of February 20, 1865, included only the troops stationed in and around the Richmond and Petersburg lines. The return is copied in Badeau's

*At this time Sheridan's cavalry had not joined Grant, and the return probably included troops at Norfolk and Fortress Monroe.

work and he comments upon it and analyzes it. That return, which was before his eyes when he wrote, shows on its face, that it included not only Lee's troops stationed around Richmond and Petersburg, but the troops as well of Early stationed in the Valley and then numbering 3,105 enlisted men, and also the troops under Walker, on the railroad defenses, numbering 1,414 enlisted men, and unattached commands numbering 504 enlisted men. Badeau assumes, indeed asserts, that the troops in the Valley and those on the Richmond and Danville defenses were used in the final defence of the Richmond and Petersburg lines. Was he so ignorant of events, of which he writes, that he did not know that over half of Early's little force in the Valley included in that return was either killed, wounded or captured in battle near Waynesboro, Virginia, with Sheridan's cavalry, on March 2, 1865? Those who escaped were disorganized, and when reorganized the greater part of them remained in the Valley—not over a fifth of the force, if that much, ever reached Lee. The troops on the Richmond & Danville Railroad, the integrity of which line of supply was so vital to Lee, and then so heavily threatened, were of course not available to guard the Petersburg lines.

Badeau's method of arriving at Lee's effective strength on 25th of March, 1865, is indeed remarkable throughout. He cites Lee's return of February 20th, 1865, which, as we have seen, included not only Lee's troops around Richmond and Petersburg, but those in the Valley, and on the railroad defenses, and some unattached commands, and says that for the "Army of Northern Virginia alone" the return shows 59,094 men present for duty, and an aggregate of 73,349. He then nearly doubles Ewell's effective strength (which it seems was not included in Lee's return of February 20th, 1865,) and adding that to the aggregate already reported gives Lee an aggregate of 78,433 on March 25th, 1865, exclusive of the naval battalion and some horse guards or local reserves. From this aggregate, in which are included all the sick, all the officers and men "on extra or daily duty," and all the officers and men in arrest, in Lee's army, Badeau subtracts only 8,433 for men not available for line of battle duty, and asserts that the residue of 70,000 is Lee's effective fighting strength!

The very return, on which Badeau bases his argument, shows that Lee, at that very time, had 5,330 officers and enlisted men sick, and 7,179 enlisted men detailed in the various staff depart-

ments, and 830 men in arrest—a total of 13,728 soldiers, as Badeau himself estimates the number—who are never counted any-
where in ascertaining the line of battle strength of any army,
except when Badeau estimate Lee's effectives. Subtract this
number, 13,728, from 78,433, the aggregate Badeau ascribes to
Lee, and Lee would have only 64,705 effectives, including the
5,169 effectives stationed in the Valley and on the railroad defences. These latter, we have seen, were not and could not be
present at the final assault on the lines. If we deduct them, Badeau's own figures, after allowing an exaggeration of Ewell's effectives, would give Lee only 58,906 effectives on March 25th, 1865.
In Vol. 3, p. 686, of the work, Badeau gives an official table,
from the Adjutant General's Office, "of the strength of the forces
under General Grant operating against Richmond from March,
1864, to April, 1865, inclusive." From the official record it appears that in March, 1865, Grant had: "Present for duty, officers,
5,288; enlisted men, 123,225; on extra or daily duty, officers, 1,060;
enlisted men, 19,731; sick, officers 77, enlisted men 5,214; in arrest, officers 77, enlisted men 510"—a grand aggregate of 155,254,
around Petersburg and Richmond. If we apply Badeau's rule for
estimating Lee's effective strength, by deducting a little over one-
eighth from this aggregate of 155,254 for men not available for
line of battle duty, and treat the residue as Grant's effective
force, it would give him over 135,000 effectives. If we deduct
from Grant's aggregate, all of his sick, extra duty men and those
in arrest (which is generally considered a fair test of the fighting
strength) it would give him 123,225 effectives on March 25th,
1865. Badeau shrank from applying this test, which he used to
ascertain Lee's effectives, because it would show that Grant had at
least 24,000 more men than Badeau gives him. He does even
worse. Grant's own returns, as we have seen, show that Grant
had at this time (after excluding all sick, extra duty men and those
in arrest, which amount to 31,996 men) 123,255 effective enlisted
men. Badeau, without so much as suggesting a reason for it, ar-
bitrarily cuts Grant's effective strength down 12,000 below what
his own returns show it to be, and puts his effective strength at
"110,000 soldiers" Evidently Badeau felt that his method of arriving at Lee's effective strength, which was so different from that
employed to ascertain Grant's, needed some bolstering up besides
the figures he gave, and, he endeavors to support it by the bald as-

sertion that the "rebels habitually put into battle nearly all" of the extra duty men. If the "rebels" could do this, it is fair to presume that Grant did it also. But it is impossible to use the bulk of the extra duty men in battle, as any experienced soldier knows. Gen. Humphreys' "Virginia Campaign, 1864–5," p. 409, speaking of such a claim, says:

"The column present for duty equipped," is intended to give the number of enlisted men that form the fighting force of the army, together with those that may be made available for it, such as the provost guard ; but does not include those on extra or daily duty who form no part of this force, *and are not available for it.*"

All the military glory in the late conflict can not be awarded to either side, and there is enough for both. Whatever feats in arms either accomplished are now the common heritage of the American people. Where numbers are material in proving the prowess of either army, writers, and especially soldiers who fought in either army, should seek to get the facts as they existed and fairly apply the same methods to both armies for arriving at the truth.

It is little to be wondered at that the statements of Badeau as to the numbers of either army, when he uses such methods to ascertain them, are generally considered as little authority by writers on both sides.

It is an indisputable historical truth that Grant's army outnumbered Lee's nearly three to one on the morning of April 1st, 1865.

CONDITION OF THE TWO ARMIES.

But comparison of numbers merely can not give any true conception of the disparity between the two armies. What the army of Northern Virginia fought in front, the world knows. What mighty obstacles fought it in the rear, the world will never know until the Confederate archives are all laid bare.

One of the greatest of philosophers has said that "in war the moral is to the physical as three to one," and when this element is considered, the disparity in numbers and equipment between the two armies shrinks into insignificance, in determining the odds against which the Army of Northern Virginia fought.

It is no vain boast or impeachment of the courage of the army of the Potomac to declare that the soldiers of the army of Northern

Virginia, standing on their own soil and in defense of their own capital, man for man, were superior to their opponents. But aside from the skill and courage of the officers and men, devotion to their cause, profound faith and love for their commander, and a proud record of glory in arms which none ever surpassed, the Army of Northern Virginia was at that time at a fearful disadvantage compared with the Army of the Potomac, not only in numbers and equipment, but in nearly all conditions and circumstances that fight with the soldier and give power and soul to armies. The winter of 1864-5 was one of marked severity, making duty of any kind very arduous. The clothing of the Confederate troops, which at best was hardly sufficient, had become threadbare and tattered, and they were often without shoes. Their food during this period consisted chiefly of corn bread, for there was little meat of any kind. Most of the bacon issued to the troops had been imported through Wilmington and other ports. The capture of these places cut off this source of supply, and when the supply on hand was exhausted little could be obtained elsewhere; for the meat in the country was about exhausted and the railroad facilities for hauling it were miserable. Medicines of the simplest kind were extremely scarce; and coffee, tea and sugar were generally rarities even in the hospital. Now and then the commissary department secured some peas and potatoes and sometimes fresh beef; and on this supply the army existed rather than lived during the winter of 1865. A soldier who received a quarter of a pound of bacon, often rancid, and a pound of flour for a day's ration considered himself most fortunate. The effect of this exposure and suffering upon the health of Lee's men, as compared with Grants, is strongly presented by the sickness in the two armies, as shown by their respective sick lists. Lee's return of February 20th, 1,865, gives 5330 sick out of an aggregate of 73,349, while Grant's returns about the same time show a sick list of 5,360 out of an aggregate of 155,224, or more than double the sickness in proportion in Lee's army than in Grant's.

General Lee himself gives a vivid and sad picture of the suffering of his army at this time, in a dispatch to the Secretary of War. Under date of 8th February, 1865, he says:

"Yesterday, the most inclement day of the winter, the troops had to be maintained in line of battle, having been in the same condition two previous days and nights. I regret to be compelled to state that under these circumstances, heightened by the assaults and fire of the enemy, some of the men have been without meat for three days, and all are suffering from reduced rations and scant clothing, exposed to battle, cold and rain. Their physical strength, if their courage survives, must fail under this treatment. Our Cavalry has to be dispersed for want of forage. Taking these facts, in connection with the paucity of numbers, you must not be surprised if calamity befalls us."

About the same time he notified the War Department that " the cavalry and artillery are scattered for want of forage, and the amunition trains are absent in North Carolina and Virginia collecting provisions," and adds, " you see to what straits we are reduced, but I trust to work out."

In a secret session of the Confederate Congress, about that time, the condition of the Confederate Commisariat was given as follows: (1) There was not enough meat in the Southern Confederacy for the armies it had in the field: (2) There was not in Virginia either meat or bread enough for the armies within her limits; (3) The supply of bread for those armies to be obtained from other places depended absolutely upon keeping open the railroad connections to the South; (4) The meat must be obtained from abroad through seaport towns: (5) The transportation was not now adequate, from whatever cause, to meet the necessary demands of the service; (6) The supply of fresh meat to Gen. Lee's army was precarious, and if the army fell back from Richmond and Petersburg, there was every probability that it would cease altogether."

It might have been added that the track and rolling stock of the railroads entering Richmond and Petersburg and their connections, were so worn that they could hardly do more than haul from day to day the necessary supplies of food and military stores to keep Lee's army in readiness for the field, much less supply the wants of the population of Richmond and Petersburg. These roads were likely to be interrupted at any time by the floods or cut by cavalry raids. The accumulation of supplies for a few days ahead was an impossibility*.

---

*As early as June 26, Gen. Lee wrote President Davis stating ' I am less uneasy about holding our position, than about our ability to procure supplies for the army." On 22nd July, 1864, he wrote the War Department, "Our supply of corn is exhausted to-day, and I am informed that the small reserve in Richmond is consumed."

The James river, on the contrary, furnished Grant a line of communication and a mode of supply which could not be cut by raids or disturbed except by ships. One gunboat on the river could defy all Lee's efforts to interrupt navigation. A wonderful merchant marine transported on the broad bosom of the river all that wealth could obtain from every quarter of the Globe to add to Grant's magazines ; while it floated a powerful navy, which not only protected his line of communication and depot of supplies at City Point, but could join at pleasure in assaults on Lee's lines near Drury's Bluff. So great were the mechanical appliances at Grant's command, that we often heard the whistle of his locomotives on a military railroad which followed within half a day in the track of his columns. So great was the dearth of the neccessaries of life among Lee's troops at this same time, that we find him writing an earnest letter to the Secretary of War in regard to procuring material with which the soldiers could make soap, for want of which there was much suffering.

Sherman's march to the sea, with its wide swath of destruction, had isolated the Army of Northern Virginia from the rest of the Confederacy and shut out even news from home from thousands of soldiers in its ranks. Hood's army had been driven from Atlanta and had battered itself to pieces in vain valor at Franklin, and then suffered rout at Nashville. Wilmington, Savannah and Charleston had fallen. The forlorn hope which Early had so long and gallantly led in the Valley of Virginia, had at last been driven from that land of historic memories. There was little of hope to sustain or cheer the grim veteran of the Army of Northern Virginia who starved and froze in the trenches, as the foe in front, whom he still beat back, fired shotted salutes into his lines to tell of victories won in other quarters.*

Grant's soldiers suffered for nothing which money or the ingenuity of man could supply, and had constant communication with homes, far from the track of war, where the munificence of a powerful government protected their families from want. They saw the circle of the hunt drawing closer around the Army of Northern Virginia, and conscious of the weight of numbers, had already caught the glow of victory and looked to the coming cam-

---

*Such salutes were fired in honor of the victories at Atlanta, Winchester, Cedar Creek, Nashville, and the capture of Charleston and Savannah, and the fall of Fort Fisher.

paign, buoyed by the hope that it would crown their labors and sacrifices with glory in arms and victorious peace.

In the other army, thinner and thinner grew its scant battallions, and wider and wider they were stretched to guard their long lines. Cold and hunger struck them down in the trenches, while from the desolate track of triumphant armies in their rear came the cries of starving and unprotected homes. From other fields, quickly succeeding each other, came the resounding crash of blows that shattered the fabric of the Confederacy all around them, save where their bayonets still upheld it. Misery sought the soldiers of the Army of Northern Virginia by every avenue through which the heart of man can be reached.

The coming campaign would only bring new and more powerful foes upon its track, while it was yet too weak to drive off the old foe in front. Even lion-hearted courage and resolve, could not shut out the thought from some, that all that they could give of life or blood might not ward off disaster. To the reflecting Confederate, the end, with all its attending miseries, indeed, seemed not far off, and the strain upon the morale of an army of less sterner stuff, would have shriveled its strength and melted it away before the shock came. And this is the crowning glory of that army that it neither faltered nor shrank even in the shadow of fate itself. Hope was well nigh hopeless. Duty and honor and the God-like bearing of its grey-haired chief alone sustained the Army of Northern Virginia during this long and desolate winter and spring. If the fickle and varying fortunes of war could not bring deliverance in the coming campaign, that army still believed it might at least wring other terms of peace than surrender at discretion. It calmly awaited the issue, and contemplated surrender only as the heroic Poniatowski, when he declared to those about him: "Now, gentlemen, it becomes us to die with honor."

About the middle of March, Sherman had established his large army about Goldsboro, North Carolina, some 145 miles south of Petersburg, and in the latter part of the month came to City Point, where he conferred with Grant. Sherman would be ready as soon as spring hardened the roads, to join his army with Grant's and make a combined attack on Lee, or he could act independently on Lee's line of communication at Burkeville Junction. One of these things he was sure to do. Johnston's small army could do no more than impede Sherman's march. Lee was too weak to drive Grant from his front, and to remain where he was was to give his only line of retreat and supply to Sherman, and thus to be ground to pieces between the upper and nether mill-stones of his adversaries. The only hope was to leave the Petersburg lines, unite with Johnston, and strike a decisive blow at Sherman before Grant could come to his assistance. This, of course, involved the evacuation of the Confederate capital, an event which Lee had long forseen and advised. For some reason the authorities at Richmond determined to postpone its abandonment to the last. Whether the Confederacy, under the circumstances, could have survived, at any time during the last two years of the war, the loss of Richmond, with the tremendous political and military consequences which must follow, is a question upon which it is now idle to speculate.

BATTLE OF HARE'S HILL, OR FORT STEADMAN.

Gen. Lee resolved to try a bold stroke to revive the failing fortunes of the Confederacy. His design was, if possible, to destroy Grant's left wing, or failing in that, to make him so contract his left as not to embarrass the passage of the Confederate column South on its way to join Johnston's army near Greensboro. He resolved to attack Grant's line at Ft. Steadman, which was near the Appomattox, about two miles distant from Petersburg. Here, the works of the two armies were about 150 yards apart, and the picket lines less than one-half that distance. This point gained, it was believed it would be easy to seize three forts on high ground that commanded Ft. Steadman and the enemy's retrenchments on the right and left of it, and thus have a vantage ground from which to destroy Grant's left wing. Three columns of infantry were to follow the assaulting party, and capture these forts, and a division of infantry moving by its flank was to follow the storming columns, and when halted and fronted was to move down Grant's lines to his left, being successfully joined by the troops in Lee's trenches as their fronts were cleared. A brigade of cavalry was held in readiness to cut through the gap at Steadman, destroy the telegraph lines and the pontoon bridges over the Appomattox and spread demoralization in the rear of the lines. Gen. Gordon was selected to command the attack, and there were put under his orders, in addition to his own corps, a portion of Hill's, and a small brig-

ade, or detachment of cavalry ; a division from Longstreet was also
to report to him. From the best information now available, the
troops put under Gordon's orders amounted to about 14,000 men.

About 5 o'clock on the morning of the 25th of March, the picket-
guard and picket line in our front were quietly seized almost without the firing of a gun, and the storming columns broke the main
line between batteries 9 and 10, and turning to the right and the
left gained battery 10, overpowered the garrison at Ft. Steadman,
capturing the greater part of it, and turned its artillery and that
in battery 10 against the enemy. Batteries 11 and 12 were also
captured. Some of our troops reached the military railroad
and telegraph about a mile and a half in rear of Ft. Steadman, but
the commander of one of the storming columns was wounded,
and the guide of another column lost his way. The forts to be
attacked were found to be of different character than at first sup-
posed, and required a change of disposition for proper attack. The result was that the attacks upon the three forts were
disjointed, and although gallantly made were repulsed with
loss. Owing to the breaking down of the railroad, or other cause,
the troops from Longstreet did not arrive on the field, in time.
Waiting for them delayed the attack nearly an hour, so that when
made the plan of operation against these forts could not be exe-
cuted before daylight, as had been intended.

The enemy after the first alarm and surprise quickly
concentrated and in an hour or so our troops were driven
into Ft. Steadman—Hare's Hill as it is called in the
Confederate accounts—and the space immediately around it,
although they had handsomely repulsed several of the first attempts to drive them from the captured works.* In this last posi-

*In a short time, probably less than an hour after the first alarm was given
Gen. Tidball, commanding the artillery of the 9th corps, concentrated a number
of field pieces on the hills in rear of Ft. Steadman, about midway between it and
Meade's Station, and opened a very savage fire. Hartranft's division which lay
in reserve, the greater portion not being more than a mile and a half in rear of
Steadman, was promptly marched to the rescue, and Gen. Hartranft, using the
first troops which came up, made at great sacrifice two attacks on our troops outside the fort, to delay their deployment. He was repulsed in these with heavy
loss, but the effort was worth all it cost. It was Tidball's fire, Hartranft's attacks
and the cross-fire of Haskell and McGilery, which prevented the timely deployment of the Confederate troops, after Ft. Steadman fell, and not any lack of spirit
of our men.

tion they were subjected to a pittiless cross-fire of artillery and small arms to which they could not effectually reply. The situation of the troops who had entered the Union lines was now desperate. Gen. Lee, who watched the battle near Cemetery Heights, concurred with Gordon that the troops must be speedily withdrawn, and the latter despatched a staff officer to the different commanders to direct their men to run back in squads and get into the Confederate lines as best they could. This was effected without any counter attack in front of Steadman. The Confederate loss in this battle was nearly thirty-five hundred, and the enemy's a little over one thousand. Gen. Gordon captured and brought back 560 men including Brig. Gen. McLaughlin and two Coehorn mortars. Thus failed a brilliant stroke which promised great results. The troops had fought with vigor and determination, and the failure of the attack was due to untoward circumstances or chance, which cannot always be guarded against in war.

THE BEHAVIOUR OF THE TROOPS.

A northern and a southern writer both take a different view of the conduct of the troops here and assert that it demonstrated a loss of their old time fire and vigor, and that they could no longer be depended upon for vigorous offensive movement.* These opinions are superficial, and based upon the erroneous accounts which at first appeared and were generally accepted as true, because the later and better information was not gathered, but actually lost

---

*Such an assertion would never have been made by any one who witnessed the bearing of the men while under fire or the conduct of the large portion of the troops on that bleak March night, as they tramped after midnight through the tombstones and graves of "the cemetery" to take position and await the order of assault. The darkness was little relieved by moon or stars. The hum of voices in this city of the dead was low, and the movement of armed bodies through it almost as noiseless and shadowy as the flitting of ghosts, while the strokes of the neighboring clocks sounded on the still night air like the tolling of funeral bells. Here were seen men tying or pinning large strips of white cloth over their breasts and shoulders, much resembling the sashes pall-bearers sometimes wear, to enable the assaulting columns to distinguish friend from foe when the enemy's works were entered. Those who thus arrayed themselves at midnight, in a graveyard, to prepare for assault, could not fail to be reminded by the solemn and wierd scene of death. The surroundings were indeed befitting a plunge into black death itself; yet none faltered or left the ranks, and the men were as cheerful as if waiting to return to their warm winter quarters. They never lost heart or courage, and were always equal to the offensive, and were still capable of anything.

sight of in the succession of disasters of greater magnitude during the next fortnight.

Gordon carried into the enemys' lines not over eight thousand troops. Those ordered from Longstreet did not arrive, the cavalry remained in its position near the old Gas Works, and a portion of Gordon's men remained in his lines to await the time when, their fronts being uncovered, they could move to the attack. The troops engaged lost over one thousand in killed and wounded—more than one-ninth their numbers. They were more than "decimated" a term often used before our late war to describe fearful losses. True, nearly two thousand unwounded men surrendered in the trenches, when retaken in the final counter-charge, made about three hours after the Confederates took Ft. Steadman. The space actually captured from the enemy at this point did not give sufficient room for the deployment of all the troops, who entered the enemys' works, to avail themselves of the expected success of the three assaulting colums. While waiting the result of the attacks on Ft. Haskell, and Ft. McGilvry, and after these were repulsed, as well as during the several assaults made by the enemy to retake the captured lines held by the Confederates, the greater portion of Gordon's men were confined in a restricted space, and to escape the pitiless enfilading fire of cannon, mortars and small arms which swept not only the flanks but both sides of the captured works, had often to seek cover in the rear of these works, or the side nearest the enemy, because the original front or side nearest Confederate lines, was literally torn up by the enemys' shot and shell. During the greater part of the three hours, elapsing between the capture and recapture of Steadman, these troops had been under this heavy fire, from which they could not find shelter and to which they could not collectively reply, and were all the while obedient to orders and displaying the most unflinching courage. *Their conduct was indeed splendid. Their situation, as we have seen, became so distressing that the officers were ordered to make their men run out of the works in squads, and get back into their own lines as best they could. It required considerable time to communicate the order from the several

---

*Gen. Lee, in a dispatch sent to the Secretary of War at 11:20 p. m. that day, says: "All the troops engaged, including two brigades under Brig. Gen. Ransom, behaved most handsomely. The conduct of the sharp-shooters of Gordon's corps, who led the assault, deserves the highest commendation."

Division Head-quarters down to the men through their respective Brigade and Regimental commanders. In several instances, staff officers bearing these orders were shot down, and the orders were not communicated and had to be repeated. The smoke and noise of the artillery, mortars and small arms, whose fire was concentrated on the few acres around Steadman occupied by the Confederate troops, was so great that it was difficult either to see or to hear at any distance. Many of the captured troops undoubtedly never received the order, and fought the enemy in front, not knowing that their comrades had left until they received a fire from the flank and rear, which cut off flight and forced surrender. Most of the commands, however, had received the order before the countercharge began, and it burst upon the Confederates just as their line of battle, in several places, was leaving the captured works, and had turned their backs upon the enemy to regain our own retrenchments. Under these circumstances, the number taken prisoners was not exceptionally large compared to the number engaged, and it does not at all sustain the verdict that the troops did not fight well, or that their morale had been so impaired that they could no longer be relied on for offensive movements.

GRANT'S COUNTER MOVEMENT.

General Meade thinking the Confederate line, owing to the concentration at Steadman, must be weak on our right, furiously attacked the Confederate lines at several places, but with the exception of the capture of an entrenched picket line in front of Gen. Wright's corps met with little success. Our loss in these affairs was about one thousand and the enemy's is believed to be about the same.

The situation of the Confederate army was now indeed disheartening, for Grant could leave as strong a force as Lee had, in Grant's works, which were stronger than Lee's, and thus hold or contain Lee within his own lines and be free to use twice Lee's numbers in the unfortified country upon his flank. To meet such a disposition of Grant's troops, which was sure to be made, Lee's only resource was to strip his already threadbare lines, leaving them to be held by a thin skirmish line, and form a column with the remainder of his troops with which to strike at the enemy's flanking columns. Grant, indeed, had already issued preparatory orders for a general movement upon Lee's right the day before the attack upon Fort Steadman.

At this time Gen. Hill held the right of Lee's line from Hatchers Run to Battery Gregg. The 2nd corps, Gordon's troops, held from Battery Gregg to the Appomattox River, while Longstreet occupied the trenches north of the Appomattox to the extreme left on White Oak Swamp. From right to left the Confederate line of works was about 37 miles in length.*

On the 28th March Sheridan was ordered to move next day with his 13,000 cavalry towards Dinwiddie Court House, attack the rear and right of Lee if practicable, while the 2nd and 5th corps, 35,000 strong together, guarded the interval between Sheridan and left of Grant's line. After this, Sheridan was instructed to cut loose and push for the Danville road and act as circumstances might require. The 2d and 5th corps, Humphreys and Warren's, were at the same time instructed to press close up to the Confederate lines, so as to keep the defending force with them and also to reach around and attack its flank if possible. Gen. Ord, commanding the Army of the James, taking half of his army from the north side of the river, in all about 19,000 men, made a secret march on the night of the 27th and took position in the rear of the 2d corps, relieving it from its position in the trenches. The 6th corps, under Gen. Wright, numbering over 19,000 men, and the 9th corps, under Gen. Parke, of about the same strength, remained in the trenches south of Petersburg, with instructions to assault if they found the force in their front greatly weakened, or if more advantageous for Parke to extend so as to allow the 6th corps to be withdrawn to join in the turning movement. A heavy rain fell on the night of the 29th, which greatly embarrassed the movements of both armies.

ACTIONS ON WHITE OAK ROAD AND AT DINWIDDIE

Lee early divining the purpose of the enemy, sent Gen'l Anderson with Bushrod Johnson's division and Wise's brigade, to the extreme right of his entrenchments along the White Oak

---

*Humphreys says, p. 310: "In the spring of 1865, when these works were completed, the Confederate entrenchments were thirty-seven miles in length from the White Oak Swamp on their left to the Claiborne road crossing of Hatcher's run on their right. This length is not measured along the irregularities of the general line of intrenchments, much less those of the parapet lines."

road, on the morning of the 29th, and Pickett's division which had been relieved from the Bermuda Hundreds by Mahone, was transferred to the same point about day-light on the 30th. Gen. Hill, commanding the Confederate corps on the right, stretched his lines still thinner so as to add to the force confronting Humphreys and Warren. Gen. Lee ordered Fitz Lee's cavalry to Five Forks, and they arrived in the vicinity of Sutherland's station on the night of the 29th, the object of the concentration being to attack Sheridan and drive him back. Pickett's Division was about 3,600 strong; Johnson's 3,000; the cavalry of the two Lee's about 4,000; making, with some other troops, a total of about thirteen thousand for the moveable column, with which Lee hoped to strike some weak place in Grant's armor, and crush his flanking force as he had so often done before.* These forces of Lee were concentrated at Five Forks on the evening of the 30th of March. Gen. Lee struck the exposed flank of the 5th corps and drove back two of its divisions with the brigades of McGowan, Gracie, Hunton and Wise, but the ground was wooded, and the 3d Division of Warren's corps coming to his assistance, the retreat of his other two divisions was stopped, while an attack by Humphrey on the left of Wise's brigade, which was the extreme left of the Confederate attacking force, compelled the retirement of the Confederate force to their intrenchments.

Foiled in the attempt to destroy the 5th corps, and paucity of numbers constraining him to be cautious, Lee next attempted the destruction of Sheridan's force, which was widely separated from the Federal infantry. Sheridan, appreciating the value of Five Forks, had temporarily taken possession of it, while the Confederate infantry had been engaged with Warren, but Lee moved Pickett and Bushrod Johnson over the White Oak road to Five Forks, and drove the Federal cavalry in disorder on Dinwiddie Court House, and isolated a portion of the force from Sheridan's main line at Dinwiddie. The Confederate infantry and cavalry then assailed Sheridan's main body at Dinwiddie C. H. and handled it severely. There is much ground for believing, as

---

*This is the best estimate I can make with the data at hand. One of Pickett's brigades had not reached him, and Anderson's whole division was not present. Of the cavalry reported February 20th, 1865, a large number were dismounted. Gen. Pickett estimates the total force as considerably less than stated in the text.

the Confederates claim, that night probably prevented the destruction of this force.

Grant on learning the situation, was very anxious about Sheridan, and subordinated all his movements to his relief. About midnight on the 31st, Pickett's position being isolated, all the troops which had been operating against Sheridan, were withdrawn to Five Forks by Gen'l Lee. Sheridan followed with the 5th corps and the cavalry under his command and about 3 o'clock in the evening of April 1st, masking the movement of the infantry by his cavalry, succeeding in getting the 5th corps in on the left of the Confederate works, and, in spite of the efforts of officers and men, almost surrounded and routed the greater portion of Pickett's and Johnson's troops, which vainly endeavored to change front to meet his attack. The Confederate loss in this action was not less than 4,700.* The fragments of Pickett's command, with some troops sent by Gen'l Lee to cover their retreat, took position at Sutherland station. The Confederate force in the trenches in the Petersburg lines was now a mere picket line, the men being from five to seven yards apart, and at dawn on Sunday the 2nd, Grant ordered Parke, Wright and Ord to assault. With the exception of three places in front of Petersburg, Gordon held his lines, but the 6th and 2d corps brushed through the cob-web force in front of them, and swept up and down the Confederate lines from Hatcher's Run to the inner lines around Petersburg. At this time Gen. Hill, who had been at Lee's headquarters, perceiving the commotion in his lines, and not knowing the extent of the disaster rode forward, and was shot dead by some of the enemy's skirmishers, who preceded an advance which was then bearing in the direction of the Turnbull house, where Gen. Lee had his headquarters. Thus fell, at a time when most needed, an heroic soldier, whose name is honored wherever the army of Northern Virginia is known. At Battery Gregg, held by a mixed command, mainly Mississippians, about two hundred and fifty strong, Ord's forces were detained an hour, and though he threw overwhelming numbers against the fort, it

---

*Col. Taylor states it 1,300 more. See discussion further on, under head "Numbers, Losses," &c., and note, as to number captured there.

did not surrender until its 250 defenders had been reduced to 30, and inflicted a loss of nearly 800 upon their assailants. This delay gave time to arrange for the defense of the inner line.

For some reason Longstreet did not perceive the weakening of the force in his front at the time of Ord's withdrawal, and hence had not moved over to the south side of the river as instructed in that event, but about 10 a. m., on April 2, some of his brigades reached Petersburg, and with these an attack was made upon the 9th corps, which together with these Gordon made, to recapture a part of his line, were so fierce that the garrison from City Point had to be ordered up. The Confederate forces now held the line from Richmond to Petersburg, and in that city, and an inner line, the right of which rested upon the Appomatox. In this position it was able to resist all attacks until darkness came to its relief.

ORDERS FOR THE RETREAT.

When the Confederate lines were carried, orders were given for the evacuation of Richmond, and the concentration of the army at Amelia Court House. Gen. Anderson was directed to move up along the Appomattox to Amelia Court House, and he was joined on the road by the remnants of Pickett's command and some troops of Hill's corps under Gen. Cooke, who handsomely repelled with severe loss two attacks on him near Sutherland's Station by Gen. Miles; but Miles was reinforced, and by a third attack succeeded in forcing these troops from the field in some confusion. The rear was covered by Fitz-Lee, whose cavalry had done brilliant service in the action at Five Forks, and in stemming the pursuit undertaken by Sheridan's cavalry after the Confederate infantry had broken.

THE MORALE OF THE TROOPS.

The troops who left the Petersburg lines on the retreat with Lee were of no ordinary mould. Each was a veteran of years of terrible war and trial, the survivor of many a bloody battle. They had experienced victories without undue elation, and bore disaster and suffering without being cast down. They remained with their colors when the faint-hearted and selfish fell by the way-side, because of a deep conviction of the justice and necessity of their cause, and were sustained by a high sense of duty and

personal pride which scorned discharge unless it came through
victory or by death or wounds. The larger portion of them had
an abiding faith, amounting almost to fanaticism, that the God of
Battles would, in the end, send their cause safe deliverance, and
they followed Lee with an almost child-like faith, which set no
bounds to his genius and power of achievement. They did not
doubt that he would unite with Johnston and destroy Sherman
and then turn on Grant; or else take up a new line and hold
Grant at bay, until the country in the rear rallied and gave Lee
power to resume the offensive. The power of the South to in-
definitely prolong the struggle by partisan war if its main armies
were compelled to disperse, was a belief fostered by the traditions
of the Revolution, and largely pervaded the ranks. It was a
general thought among these men that long continued resistance, and the burdens it would entail upon the invader, as well
as the blows of Confederate arms, would finally wring recognition
and peace from the United States. Such was the frame of mind of
most of these men as they turned their backs upon the Confederate
capital; and while they were too intelligent not to appreciate the
extent of the disaster, they entered upon the retreat with good
heart and undoubted morale. The men had been so long cooped
up in the trenches, that their march into the open fields and woods,
on the night of April 2d. was as exhilarating to them as cool
breezes and sun-light to one long confined in the close air of a dark
dungeon. These things explain the almost bouyant spirit of
Lee's troops on that fateful night. The belief that the retreat
would possibly end in surrender entered the minds of few.
While the final result would probably not have been altered if
Lee had made a junction with Johnston, it is certain if there had
been food to sustain the bodies of these men, their unquenched
courage would have written a different history for the retreat
from the Petersburg lines.

MOVEMENTS TO APRIL 5TH.

Longstreet crossed the Appomattox at Pochahontas Bridge,
and moved along the north side of the river. intending to
re-cross at Bevil's Bridge, but that being out of repair,
used the pontoon at Goode's Bridge. Gordon taking the
Hickory road, re-crossed at Goode's Bridge, and Kershaw

and Custis Lee's divisions, comprising Ewell's command at Richmond, crossed the James at Richmond and moving on the Genito road followed by Gary's cavalry, crossed the Appomattox on the Danville Railroad Bridge. Grant sent Sheridan and the 5th corps to move on the south side of the river, to follow Lee's army and strike the Danville road between its crossing of the Appomattox and the crossing of the Lynchburg road at Burkville Junction. Gen. Meade himself, with the 2nd and 6th corps, followed with the same general instructions, and Ord's command was ordered to move along the south side of the railroad to Burkeville Junction, followed by the 9th corps.

It will be seen that the 5th infantry corps and Sheridan's cavalry, on the morning of the 3rd were in position to cut off Lee's retreat by the south bank of the Appomattox.

Longstreet reached Amelia Court House on the afternoon of the 4th. Gordon's command was three or four miles distant, and Mahone's division was still near Goode's Bridge. Ewell's command arrived about 12 o'clock, and Anderson and Fitz-Lee's cavalry on the morning of the 5th. For some reason the expected supplies at Amelia were not there, and hunger and fatigue told fearfully upon the men who had but one ration since the retreat commenced. In order to obtain food foraging parties were sent out, and Lee was detained at Amelia on the 4th, and a large part of the 5th of April. Thus precious time was lost and the last opportunity to strike at Grant's widely scattered pursuing columns. Meanwhile, Sheridan, on the afternoon of the 4th, had struck the Danville road at Jetersville, seven miles southwest of Amelia C.H. and entrenched. Lee's infantry at this time did not amount to 25,000 fighting men, and as Sheridan's cavalry was entrenched at Jetersville and had been reinforced by the 5th corps, it equalled, if it did not exceed Lee's whole army, and Lee, who had advanced towards Jetersville on the afternoon of the 5th with the view of attacking Sheridan, if he had not been too heavily reinforced by infantry, had no alternative but to attempt to march around him. Lee still hoped that by a vigorous right march westward, he might get far enough in advance to reach Lynchburg, by passing through Deatonsville, Rice's Station and Farmville, and perhaps get to Danville.

NO FOOD AT AMELIA.—TRIALS OF THE RETREAT.

The disappointment at not finding the expected supplies at
Amelia threw a great damper upon the spirits of the famishing
troops; but they did not quail but only girded their loins the
tighter to meet the fearful ordeal ahead of them. When the
army moved, after the inevitable halt at Amelia, it was to pass
through a circle of fire. An immense amount of war material
had accumulated at Richmond and Petersburg, and if the army
was to have another campaign much of it must be transported in
wagons; for the Confederates had no other suppplies and without
them the army was lost. The country roads on which these
trains must move were narrow, rough and softened by the heavy
spring rains. Every rivulet had swollen into a stream and every
little creek needed to be bridged. The immense caravan of
wheels converted every depression in the roads into a hole and
turned the roads into a perfect sea of mud through which the
supply trains and amunition wagons, artillery and ambu-
lances struggled on to reach dry land beyond, almost as vainly
as Pharoah's army in the Red Sea. Although the trains moved
on different roads and the wagons were driven two and three
abreast wherever practicable, they were often longer than
the line of the troops which marched on their flank for
their protection.* A formidable cavalry force swarmed upon the
flanks and sometimes the front and rear was attacked by infantry.
The shield of protection for these trains, which the marching
troops could afford was thin indeed, and constant thrusts at
it by the cavalry soon exposed its weak points. Through these
the cavalry charged spreading death and dismay among the sick
and wounded and helpless throngs which accompanied the trains.†

---

*Sheridan's cavalry, including McKenzie, numbered over 15,000 effective offi-
cers and men on 29th March. This force made more than three times the number of effective Confederate cavalry at that time.

†Humphreys says, p. 375: "The roads were very heavy owing to the copious
rains, and in fact were *nearly impassible* for wagon trains." The horses and
mules were in very low condition from the winter's exposure and scant provender,
and, having little forage on the retreat, were constantly falling in harness from
exhaustion and weakness. There was almost sure to be a serious delay from this
cause whenever the trains reached a steep hill or a muddy lane. Horses and men
alike, in the last days of the retreat, fell from exhaustion and misery and perished
on the road-side. With them were often mingled dead and dying soldiers who
fell in attempting to defend the trains against cavalry, which dashed in to attack
wherever the wagons moved without heavy escort.

Many times the first warnings the infantry had of these dashes was the explosion of ammunition and the smoke of burning wagons. The rear guard resisted to the last from every advantageous hill and every coin of vantage, to gain time for the balky trains to move on. Often it was driven from position while the long trains were not yet out of sight and the enemy's batteries thundered forth destruction into the trains which, spread out for miles in the road, presented a tempting mark at which not a shot could be thrown in vain. During the last days of the retreat, attack came from every quarter and the days and nights alike were spent in marching and fighting. There was not time or opportunity for sleep and of food there was none. Suspense, despair, exposure, famine, and want of sleep caused many whose weak bodies could not sustain their dauntless souls to lie down on the road side to await the coming of death. Many were not strong enough to carry their muskets and placed them in the wagon trains while they marched beside them, hoping that food and rest, when these could be obtained, would again enable them to bear arms.

On the morning of the 6th, the army of the Potomac, which had been mainly concentrated at Jetersville, moved northward to Amelia C. H. to give battle to Lee, but he had passed, as we have seen, on the night before on the Deatonsville road. Humphrey's 2nd corps was ordered to move on the Deatonsville road, and the 5th and 6th corps in parallel directions on the right and left. The Army of the James, under Ord, had in the meantime, reached Burkeville, and on the 6th Gen. Ord was directed towards Farmville. Meade discovered Lee's withdrawal from Amelia before reaching that point, and made new dispositions for pursuit. The 2nd corps soon came up with Gordon in the rear and a sharp, running fight commenced with Gordon's corps, which continued nearly all day. An obstinate stand was made at Sailor's Creek, but the numbers of the enemy enabled them to turn Gordon's position, and take some high ground commanding it, and just at night-fall his position was carried with a loss of a battery, several hundred prisoners and hundreds of wagons, which had become blocked up at the crossing of the creek near Perkinson's Mill. The 6th corps meantime had come up with Ewell, and while the cavalry detained it in the rear and on the flank, it was attacked and surrounded by the 6th corps and, after one of the most gallant fights of the war, compelled to surrender. Ewell had about 9000 men all told, and about 6000 of these were killed, wounded or captured, including Gen. Ewell and five other general officers made prisoners. Gen. Read, of Ord's staff, with Col. Washburn and a force of 80 cavalry and about 500 infantry, had been sent to destroy the high bridge, but they were intercepted about mid-day on the 6th by Rosser and Mumford, and after a severe fight in which Read and Washburn were killed and number of the men also, the remainder surrendered.

Gordon's command reached this side of High Bridge, near Farmville, that night. Longstreet, whose command had halted all that day at Rice's Station to enable the other corps to unite with them, marched that night on Farmville, and on the morning of the 7th moved out on the road passing through Appomattox C. H. and Lynchburg. Here rations were issued for the first time since the 2d April.* Gordon's troops and Mahone's crossed the High Bridge on the morning of the 7th. The 2d corps (Humphrey's) followed hard behind Gordon. Four miles north of Farmville, Gen'l Lee being hotly pressed, chose a favorable position covering the stage and plank roads to Lynchburg, threw up temporary breastworks and brought batteries in position. Humphreys attacked, but was repulsed with considerable loss. Sheridan that day sent his cavalry to Prince Edward C. H., with the exception of one division which was sent to Farmville. On the night of the 7th Lee marched nearly all night, and was followed by the 2d and 6th corps of the army of the Potomac up the north bank of the Appomattox, while Sheridan, followed by Ord and the 5th corps, advanced by the south bank and struck Appomattox station on the Lynchburg road.

On the evening of the 8th, Lee's advance was in the vicinity of Appomattox C. H., and there was reason to fear that the enemy's formidable cavalry force would reach it first and intervene between Lee and Lynchburg road, which was the only outlet left the Confederate commander. Longstreet's command was in the rear, closely pressed by Meade's army. Between Longstreet and Gordon was an innumerable caravan of wagons, artillery, disabled and unarmed men.

---

*The advance of the enemy was so close that the wagons could not be held long enough to supply many of the troops.

THE NIGHT BEFORE THE SURRENDER.

Near dusk on the 8th of April, Sheridan's cavalry, on the out-
skirts of Appomattox court house, captured several pieces of artillery, which were moving without escort ahead of the army, on
the road to Lynchburg, and several train loads of supplies sent to
feed Lee's army. Our infantry was not yet up, and worn and scattered as the troops were after a long march, it was impossible to
concentrate sufficient force to attack that night.* Whatever was
in front must be driven in the morning, for our army was now on
the narrow strip of country between the Appomattox and James
rivers, and the road to Lynchburg was the only line of retreat.

Lee resolved to cut through Sheridan's force, and Gordon, who
had for several days covered the rear, was ordered to the front to
head the movement. All that remained of the old second
corps and of Ewell and Anderson's troops were sent to him.
Mahone was to move on the left of our line of march, pro-
tecting it and the trains. Col. Thos. H. Carter, with a number
of his best guns, was to support the attack of Gordon, while Fitz-
hugh Lee who had been recently assigned to the command of all
the cavalry was to move with the cavalry on the infantry right.
Longstreet was to protect the wagon train and hold back the
enemy in the rear. The column of attack thus made up to cut
through Sheridan consisted of about two thousand five hundred
muskets and about 2,200 cavalry. Upon this force depended the
salvation of the army.†

---

*Gen. Lindsay Walker's artillery was attacked on the evening of the 8th near
Appomattox Station, but the attack was repulsed. Some of the enemy's cavalry
dashed in that same evening near the court-house, but were held in check by some
of our cavalry.

†Gen. Humphreys, who compiles the figures from official records, states the
number of cavalry paroled at Appomattox at 1786. Long makes it about two
hundred less. The estimate above gives about four hundred more. The cavalry
cut through on the 9th, and some of them left for their homes, after it was known
the army had surrendered, without waiting to be paroled with their commands
when Gen. Fitz Lee surrendered the cavalry a short time afterwards. Gen.
Robt. E. Lee, in his letter announcing the surrender to President Davis, says, "I
have no accurate report of the cavalry, but believe it did not exceed 2,100 effective
men." Hence, I have felt justified in estimating the number participating in the
action on the morning of April 9th, as greater than the number paroled.

"Gordon's Corps" at Appomattox included the old 2d corps and what was left
of Anderson and Ewell's commands, and surrendered 6,773 enlisted men, including

28

The tired Confederates sank down to rest just as they halted.
The troops had neither food nor sleep, and were too weak and
weary to build fires.

THE ATTEMPT TO CUT OUT.

About half past five, on Sunday April 9th, Gordon who had
formed his command nearly a half a mile from the court-house,
advanced his line. A proud array it was, although the men were
so worn, jaded and famished, that many could hardly carry their
muskets. Divisions had dwindled to the number of full regiments
and regiments and companies were represented by a few files of
men ; but the colors of nearly all of the organizations remained.*
The sharp skirmish fire soon grew into a furious and heavy
volume of musketry. The ever faithful Carter joined in with his
deep toned guns. The cavalry on our right pressed forward at a
gallop, and wild and fierce shouts resounded throughout the heav-

the detailed men of all the various organizations composing the corps, such as
teamsters, ordnance, ambulance drivers, etc. The detailed men amounted to at
least 1,500, for we had not only the usual proportion for the force present, but considerably more, since the detailed men of Ewell and Anderson's forces, which
were so terribly handled at Sailor's Creek, were not captured in the same proportion as its fighting strength. Deducting the number of detailed men, who are not
available for line of battle duty, would give Gordon about 5,000 infantry men.
Over half of these were too weak to bear their muskets and 40 rounds of ammunition. The strength of the infantry under Gordon in the attack is therefore placed
at "about 2,500," which corresponds with the recollection of Gen. Gordon and
other officers at the time.

*That this statement is not an exaggeration becomes quite evident when we
take the number paroled and bear in mind that it includes the detailed men, and
that over half the infantry were too weak to bear arms on the morning of April
9th. The 2d corps, composed of the divisions of Grimes, Early and Gordon,
paroled 4,456 enlisted men, exclusive of provost guard, &c., their numbers being
respectively 1,727, 1,117 and 1,612. Deducting 60 per cent. of this number for detailed men, not available for battle, and the proportion of men who were physi-
cally unable to bear arms, these *divisions* were represented in the column of attack about as follows: Grimes', 688 muskets; Early's, 444; Gordon's, 644,--none
of them having more than the strength of a full regiment. In the second corps
alone some sixty-four regimental organizations were represented, and, as the
figures show, they did not average thirty muskets in line. The showing in the
cavalry was about the same. While the corps lost some flags in battle, and fre-
quently when regiments became exceedingly small they did not carry their colors
in line, yet the number of colors carried that day, including those of Anderson's
troops, was out of all proportion to the number of men, and made the line appear
"almost scarlet."

ens. As the sun drove away that Sunday morning mist, it looked
down upon a scene that will forevermore thrill Southern hearts.
In a steady line, sustained on the left by artillery, which flamed
forth at every step, with cavalry charging fiercely on the right,
the Confederate line of battle, scarlet almost from the array of
battle flags floating over it, went forth to death, driving before
it masses of blue cavalry and artillery.* Spring was just budding
forth, and the morning sun glistening from budding leaf and tree,
shed a halo about the red battle flags with the starry cross, as if
nature would smile on the nation that was dying there. We
pressed on and beyond the court house. Fitz Lee and his
cavalry rode unmolested on the Lynchburg road, but Gordon's
infantry was impeded by a desperate resistance. Gordon's men
captured a battery, and still pressed on. It was too late. The
"infantry under Ord" nearly 30,000 strong, now filed across our
pathway, throwing out batteries from every knoll, and rapidly
advanced lines of infantry against us.† Gordon could not withstand what was in front, and to stop to resist it, would be to in-
volve his flank and rear in clouds of enemies. Slowly this glorious
color guard of the "Army of Northern Virginia" retraced it steps
to Appomattox C. H , bringing with it prisoners and captured
artillery. The probable success of Gordon's movement and what
was to be done in event of failure, had been the subject of discussion between Gen. Lee and his corps commanders. While
Gordon was falling back he received a notification from Gen. Lee
that he had sent a flag through the lines to seek an interview
with Gen. Grant, and Gordon thereupon sent flags which Sheridan
and Ord received asking a cessation of hostilities in his front until the meeting could be had.

While this was going on, Longstreet had been closely pressed
by the troops in rear and flags of truce were also sent out from his
lines requesting a cessation of hostilities on Gen'l Meade's front.

*Sheridan says his cavalry fell back slowly in accordance with orders. Ord
says, "in spite of Sheridan's attempts the cavalry was falling back in confusion
before Lee's infantry." Crook says, "the cavalry was forced to retire by overwhelming numbers until relieved by infantry, when we reorganized." Merritt
and Custer say the same thing

†Gen. Ord thinks his advance was made about ten o'clock. It was, however, a
few minutes after 9 o'clock.

Lee's last prop had fallen from under him when Gordon was driven back, and surrender was all that was left. It is not practical within the limits of an address like this to describe all the events connected with the surrender. Its minutest incidents have already passed into history, which has long since exploded the stories of the "famous apple tree," and the tender by Lee of his sword and Grant's refusal to receive it.

Whether he fought with the defeated or the victorious army, no American citizen can forget that Grant was generous in the hour of victory, and "displayed the delicacy of a great soul" in dealing with his former foes, nor that Lee on that fateful day showed how "sublime it is to suffer and grow strong," and gave to the world an example of greatness in the hour of adversity that honors the American name forever more. I will not attempt to describe what ensued on Lee's return to his own lines when it was known that all was over. No pen or tongue can tell what he and the men who crowded around him felt, or picture the scene as he turned to leave them to go to his tent. Never before had unsuccessful leader received such homage from his surrendered legions, or more respect from his foes.

Grant's army made other captures here which are often forgotten. In the actions on the Petersburg lines, the affair near the High bridge in which Read's force was destroyed, and that in which Gen. Gregg was captured, and in other combats in the retreat, Lee's army had plucked from its pursuers and safely guarded to Appomatox over fourteen hundred prisoners, including a battery of artillery and a Brigadier General of cavalry. These prisoners of the Army of Northern Virginia were of course freed by its surrender. The number of casualties in Grant's army from the commencement of the final movement to the surrender, which according to official reports amounted to 9,994 officers and men—or near one fourth of the Confederate strength at the beginning of the final struggle —bears striking testimony to the high courage of the retreating army. Its heroic endeavors are made still more conspicuous by the fact that the army of Northern Virginia, encumbered as it was with immense trains, moving over bad country roads, perishing from exposure and lack of food, and fighting daily a vastly superior force, marched, on the routes taken by it, in the six days

from the night of April 2 to the morning of the 9th over eighty-
five miles, or an average of about fourteen miles a day. Such
marches of an army of its size, under such circumstances, have
few if any parallels in military annals.

On the 10th of April officers made out muster-rolls of their
commands in duplicate and then signed and gave them paroles,
on printed blanks which had been struck off by the force of prin-
ters gathered up from the head-quarters of the various
Federal corps commanders. The Confederate troops then
marched, brigade at a time, past an equal number of Federal
troops, commanded, if my memory is not at fault, by Gen. Cham-
berlain, and stacked arms and banners. The Federal troops often
presented arms to their foes, and uniformly treated them with
the utmost respect. With this simple ceremony the surrender
was over.

NUMBERS—LOSSES—WHAT THEY PROVE.

Lee's army, as will be remembered, numbered not over fifty
thousand men of all arms when Grant commenced operations on
the 29th of March. Lee lost in killed, wounded, captured and
stragglers at least seven thousand men in the battle at Five Forks,
and the encounters at other places on the 30th and 31st March,
and the general assault on the lines on the morning of April 2nd
cost Lee, from the same causes, at least seven thousand more; so
that he had only thirty-six thousand men of all arms for duty, including 2.500 dismounted cavalry, the artillery and the mounted
cavalry, Ewell's command and the naval battalion, on the night
of April 25th, or morning of the 3d, to take upon the retreat. He
left the Petersburg line with about 26,000 infantry.

In the desperate fighting of April 6th, when Ewell and Anderson's commands were captured, and when Gordon, after engaging
in a running fight for nearly 14 miles, was driven across Sailor's
Creek. Lee lost about eight thousand men, including stragglers
who were not captured. The cavalry was constantly fighting for
the protection of the wagon trains, and so was a portion of the
infantry after the army left Amelia Court-House. There was
also the action at Sutherland's Station, April 2d; that at High
Bridge, in which Reid's force was captured, and the fighting around
Farmville, including the repulse of Humphrey, the affair in which

Gen. Gregg was captured, and also the action on the 9th at the Court-House. The losses in all the actions which took place after the retreat was begun amounted to at least 12,000 men, and subtracting that number from the force with which Lee left the Petersburg lines would leave about 24,000 men of all arms to be accounted for at Appomattox, exclusive of the force for Richmond and Danville defences of about 1,400 men. Some of this force joined Lee on the retreat and accompanied him to Appomattox, and if all are properly included in the number of troops to be accounted for there, it would make the total number 25,400. The total number surrendered at Appomattox, according to Gen. Humphreys was 28,536, and according to the figures furnished from the Adjutant General's office 27,416. This excess of between two and three thousand above the fighting force which the returns would give Lee, is accounted for by the fact that detailed men in the medical, ordnance, quartermaster, subsistence, engineer and provost departments of Lee's own army, who were not included in his line of battle strength, and some of the men detailed in the arsenals and various departments at Richmond who took part in the retreat, were also paroled at Appomattox. Any one conversant with the proportion that such details bear to the aggregate strength of an army will readily admit that this is a moderate estimate for the number of these non-combatants.

These facts and figures effectually dispute the assertions which are sought to be palmed off as the truth of history that Lee's army melted away along the retreat by regiments and scattered to their homes in advance of their pursuers.

The fact, so well known to numbers of the survivors of the Army of Northern Virginia, that Lee had not quite eight thousand organized infantry with arms in their hands on the morning of April 9th, has been disputed or doubted by Northern writers, but its correctness is susceptible of most convincing proof. It will be remembered that in the last return of Lee's army 5,155 were artillery and 5,700 were cavalry. Owing to the fact that nearly one-half of the cavalry were dismounted, and remembering their losses in the actions in which they were engaged up to the 9th, it is safe to estimate Lee's effective cavalry at between two thousand and twenty-two hundred. This exceeds the number paroled, but Fitz Lee's cavalry cut through on the morning of the 9th, and a portion left for their homes, after learning of the surrender, without waiting to be paroled when the cavalry surrendered shortly afterwards. Two thousand five hundred and eighty-six artillery men were paroled. The cavalry and artillery on the morning of the 9th, therefore, numbered about forty-seven hundred men. As the number of troops with which Lee started on the retreat was 36,000 of all arms, and the losses were 12,000, it would leave Lee 24,000 of his line of battle strength of all arms on the day of the surrender. Deduct from this number forty seven hundred for artillery and cavalry, and it would give Lee 19.300, or if we include Walker's command, 20,700 infantry on the morning of the surrender. Is it any wonder that more than half of this number had not the strength to bear their muskets? It must be remembered, also, that the greater portion of Lee's troops had been fighting and marching, during most miserable weather, since the 25th day of March, and that the whole of his force had been marching and fighting every day since the 1st day of April, and that during this trying period the troops had been without sufficient food most of the time, and for the last five days without food of any kind, sustaining themselves on leaves and twigs of the budding vegetation and a few ears of Indian corn left in the fields when the crops were gathered. This continuous exposure, fatigue, loss of sleep, and hunger, and the mental strain which the troops underwent, told fearfully upon them, and thousands of the infantry, whose courage was unquenched, were too weak to bear their muskets and had either to place them in the wagons or abandon them on the wayside. So it was that over half of them were too weak to bear arms on the morning of the 9th, and Lee could then muster not quite eight thousand organized infantry with arms in their hands, for the operations on the front, flanks and rear of his army, while Gordon and Fitz Lee attempted to cut out. Gen. Lee, in his report to President Davis of the surrender, says: "On the morning of the 9th, according to the reports of the ordnance officers, there were 7,892 organized infantry with arms, with an average of 75 rounds of ammunition per man."* The wonder, under all the circumstances, is not that he had so few, but that he had so many muskets in line.

---

*Humphreys does not deny the statement, or attempt to refute it. He remarks, if the statement is true, many of the infantry must have thrown away their muskets after the surrender became known. If documentary evidence existed, as to the

It will be noticed that the estimate of Lee's losses, from the 29th
of March to April 9th, exceeds the number of prisoners, which

number of men surrendered with arms in their hands at Appomattox, a writer of
Humphreys' ability and great research, who had the aid of the War Department
in making his investigations, would surely have found the evidence and cited it.

Publications as to the number of armed men Lee surrendered, as will be seen
from the extract below, had come to Gen. Grant's attention. He does not attempt
to refute or deny them. He says "when Lee finally surrendered at Appomattox,
there were only 28,356 officers and men left to be paroled, *and many of these were
without arms*. It was probably this latter fact [that many were without arms]
which gave rise to the statement sometimes made, North and South, that Lee surrendered a smaller number of men than what the official figures show."—Memoirs, Vol. 2, p. 500.

Badean, however, attempts to be equal to the emergency. In a note of a singular
venom and malignity, for a soldier writing fifteen years after the close of the war,
he says:

"Every rebel who has written about Appomattox, declares that only 8,000 of
those who surrendered bore arms—a statement which would not be creditable to
them if true. But as every rebel who was at Appomattox was himself a prisoner,
the assertion is worthless. The fact is that 22.633 small arms were surrendered;
and Lee did not carry many extra muskets around on wagons during the retreat
from Petersburg." Vol. 3, p. 624.

One would infer from this paragraph that there were official reports, showing
the number of small arms surrendered *at* Appomattox. If any such exist they
have not yet been found, and the documentary evidence to which Badean refers,
so far from disputing the Confederate statements, tends strongly to confirm them.
Badean, vol. 3, p. 714 of his work, publishes the following:

"STATEMENT OF CANNON AND SMALL ARMS SURRENDERED TO THE UNITED
STATES FROM APRIL 8TH, TO DECEMBER 30TH, 1865.

Date of Report	Where Surrendered.	Cannon	Small Arms.	Remarks.
April 11, 1865.	Army of the James............	263	10,000 ⎱	Lee's Army.
May 31, 1865..	Army of the Potomac	251	22.633 ⎰	

  * * * * [Here follow other places outside of Virginia.]

The records of the ordnance office do not show from what General the surrendered arms, etc., were received, except in the case of Johnston's army to Gen.
Sherman. Ordnance office, War Department, Dec. 30th, 1880."

The army of the James and the army of the Potomac were both under Grant in
all his final movements and at Appomattox. There was little fighting or even
skirmishing on the 8th of April, and no captures. The surrender took place next
day, and it ended the war. Neither of these armies took part in any more fighting,
and hence could not make any captures of arms after the 9th. It is inevitable, if
these reports cover arms actually captured between the 8th of April and their
respective dates, April 11th, May 31st, 1865, [instead of arms gathered up at Appomattox and other places in Virginia by ordnance officers of those armies between
those dates] that the captures were made at Appomattox and on the day before—
ince there was no other time or place when captures could be made between

official records show Grant captured during that period, by nearly
seven thousand men. Grant, in his Memoirs, states the number

those dates. The "statement" covers the cannon and small arms; and if, as Badeau assumes, it proves the number of small arms surrendered at Appomattox, it
equally proves the number of "cannon" surrendered. On Badeau's theory, the
statement on its face shows that 514 cannon and 32,633 small arms were surrendered at Appomattox. I have omitted from this statement the number of cannon
reported September 12th, 1865, as surrendered at "Richmond and Petersburg,"
because the report does not include any small arms, and even Badeau would
hardly contend that it referred to cannon captured at Appomattox.

Why should Badean reject one of the returns, instead of taking both ? If his
version is correct, that the reports cover arms actually captured after April 8th, he
is certainly bound to take the report of April 11th, as showing a part of the small
arms surrendered at Appomattox, for between those dates the army of the James
had been nowhere except at Appomattox and its vicinity; and there can be no
reason for not adding that number to the small arms shown in the report of
May 31st. Why he does not include the number in both reports, but rejects the
first and takes the second, we will see presently.

There are certain well known historical facts, which even Badean can not dispute. Lee at no one time during the existence of the army of Northern Virginia, had as many as 514 pieces of field artillery. That number is about double
the highest number he ever had. It is twice the number Lee had at the opening
of hostilities in the Wilderness in May, 1864, or in March, 1865, when Grant began
his final operations. Besides, Lee lost some field pieces at Five Forks, when the
Petersburg lines were swept to Hatchers run, at Sailors creek and other places
on the retreat, to say nothing of the number of pieces dismantled and destroyed by
Lee's order on the retreat, and those sent on ahead of the army. Lee himself
reported to President Davis that he had only 63 field pieces at Appomattox. It is
preposterous, therefore, to ask anybody to believe that Lee surrendered at Appomattox more field pieces than he had when he left Petersburg, and twice as many
as his army ever had. So, if it is proper construction that these two reports are
intended to give the number of "cannon" captured at Appomattox, it is proved
by undisputable historical evidence, that they are monstrously false as to the
number of "cannon," at least.

How stands the case as to the 32,633 small arms reported, if Badeau's version is
correct, and "Lee did not carry many extra muskets in wagons ?" All these small
arms, on Badeau's idea, must also have been captured at Appomattox, for as we
have seen, there was no other place between the 8th of April and the dates of the
reports where any captures could be made by either Meade's or Ord's army. If
these small arms were captured at Appomattox, how did they get there ? Lee
surrendered only 28,536 officers and men at Appomattox. Of this number at least
5,500 were officers and detailed men, teamsters, etc., who did not carry muskets.
This left only 23,000 men to bring 32,000 muskets to Appomattox, if every soldier
whose duty it was to bear arms had been able to do so. It is not pretended that
any of the infantry carried two muskets, or denied that many were unable to carry
one. The 9,000 excess of muskets, if both reports are included in getting the number of small arms, is what disturbed Badean; and he illogically rejects one report,

at 19,132, and the records of the Adjutant General's office give the same figures. The difference in number must consist in the

and then takes the other solely because the number of small arms the latter reports will not exceed the whole number of officers and men captured at Appomattox.

There is much reason for believing that the report of April 11th, the date when the last of Lee's troops stacked arms before Ord's men, and which if Badeau's version is correct could not possibly have included small arms captured elsewhere, gives the number of small arms surrendered by Lee's troops at Appomattox C. H. and that it is, perhaps, slightly in excess of the number of both cavalry and infantry who bore arms on the morning of the 9th of April.

Ord's troops, the army of the James, arrested our progress beyond the court house on the morning of the 9th, and were on the immediate vicinity of the court house where our troops stacked arms before some of his, after the paroles were made out. Gen. Gibbon, one of Ord's corps commanders, was the ranking officer charged with seeing to the formal surrender. Ord's ordnance officers quite naturally received the stacked muskets and the small arms of the cavalry, and reported them as surrendered to that army, and also included in their captures of "cannon," field pieces taken by his troops on the retreat, and siege pieces on the part of the entrenchments taken by Wietzel, his other corps commander, who entered Richmond.

Meade's infantry was in our rear at Appomattox, over three miles from the court house. His ordnance officers doubtless gathered from the trains, which were nearest his troops, all small arms found in the wagons which remained to us. In the short interval elapsing between the retreat and the hour when orders were given for it, the ordinance officers gathered up some muskets of the sick and wounded about Petersburg and put them in wagons which started with the trains; and after leaving Amelia many of the exhausted infantry rather than abandon their arms put them in the wagons. It is true that hundreds and hundreds of these wagons were captured or destroyed in the retreat at Sailors Creek, Painesville and Farmville, but it is probable that a few of these wagons reached Appomattox—and, therefore, that some small arms were taken from the wagons there. Meade's corps had made large captures of men with arms in their hands, when the Petersburg lines were broken, and at Five Forks and at Sailor's Creek His ordnance officers gleaned these battle fields, and cared for the arms. His provost marshals after his return from Appomattox, required citizens who had arms to turn them over. The aggregate of all the arms thus obtained was naturally reported by Meade's ordnance officers as surrendered to his army; and they as naturally included in the number of "cannon" not only field pieces taken at Appomattox and on the retreat, but heavy artillery on the part of the line captured by Meade's troops.

It is quite plain, therefore, that these reports of the ordinance officers, cited by Badean, were intended to give the number of small arms and "cannon" which came into their hands between the 8th of April and the date of the making of these reports, without any reference to the particular place or the number at such place, where the "cannon" and small arms were actually captured. In no other way can their truth be maintained, or the large numbers of "cannon" and small arms, reported captured, accounted for. If there could be any doubt about this, Gen. Grant himself makes it plain. In his Memoirs, Vol. 2, p. 500, he speaks as

killed, and the "missing" who were not captured; since the wounded, as well as the unwounded, who fell into the enemy's hands, were enumerated among the prisoners.

As to the battle of Five Forks I have adopted Col. Taylor's estimate, although it is greater by far than developed by the subsequent proof in the Warren Court of Inquiry, where everything connected with that battle was elaborately investigated*. The official reports show that not over 4,500 prisoners were captured there and that our killed and wounded were about 1,200.

Nevertheless, a number of men were without rations, and lost their way in the darkness and the demoralization of the rout, and were prevented by the subsequent movement of the armies from rejoining their commands, if they desired to do so. Judging by the strength of their commands next day, and sifting contem-

---

a matter "of official record" of prisoners captured "between March 29th and the date of the surrender," and then says "the same record shows the number of cannon, *including those at Appomattox*, to have been 689, between the dates named." This is the exact number of "cannon" included in those reports given in the official statement which Badeau relies on—to-wit, 263, 251 and 175—total, 689.

All in all, these two reports of captured small arms, in view of the well known facts referred to, go strongly to prove that the number of infantry surrendered, with arms in their hands, was about as stated by Confederate writers, and, more important than all, by Gen'l Robert E. Lee himself.

Badeau, evidently much worried by this statement, assails it in another note, vol. 3, p. 607. He says Lee, when asked by Grant the number of rations needed for his army, replied that he could not tell—among other reasons—because no returns "had been made for several days." Yet Badeau goes on to say "in spite of this statement of his chief," Taylor speaks of the men "who in line of battle, on 9th day of April, 1865, were reported present for duty." But Lee did not say that no returns had been *made*. Gen. Porter of Grant's staff, gives Lee's exact words: "I have not *seen* any *returns for several days*." This conversation took place on the 9th. On the 12th, three days later, Lee had evidently seen returns, for on that day he wrote his official report of the surrender, in which he says "according to the reports of the ordnance officers, there were 7,892 organized infantry with arms," &c. Ordnance officers were required to issue a full supply of ammunition to the infantry before the line advanced on the 9th, and this is probably the time when they ascertained the number of men needing it (men with arms in their hands) upon which were based the reports of which Gen. Lee speaks. This is quite a different report from the returns of the strength of the commands which comes through the Adjutant General's, and not through the Ordnance Department.

*It seems both the Cavalry Corps and Warren's in some instances claimed the capture of the same prisoners, and the official reports of both corps therefore show a much larger number of prisoners than were actually taken.

poraneous accounts, it is safe to say that 1,300 men above those killed, wounded and captured, were lost to Lee as the result of that battle. The same observations apply with like force to the losses at places where the trenches around Petersburg were carried at the break of day, and in the rout at Sailors Creek, after Gordon's persistent stand there just at dusk on April 6th, and when Ewell's and Anderson's forces were captured. Our losses there can be fairly put at more than the number of killed, wounded and captured reported by the enemy, for they do not include stragglers who did not fall into their hands, but failed to join their commands. What is the number of Lee's killed, which must be deducted from the excess above the number captured to ascertain the number of these absentees from other causes than death, captivity or wounds? Grant's losses in the final operations were 9,994 officers and men, of whom about 2,000 were killed. The Confederate loss in killed was somewhat greater. At Five Forks, at several places on the lines, and at Sailors Creek, the Confederates retreated under fire, after being defeated in battle, and sometimes in great disorder, and their losses were greater than their assailants. Grant's troops, however, fell back under fire in Warren's fight, so did Sheridan's towards Dinwiddie. Grant's troops were repulsed at several places on the lines, gained costly success at Battery Gregg* and made unsuccessful attacks on field breastworks at Sutherland's Station, and when Humphreys attacked Lee near Farmville. In these actions Grant's losses were considerably greater than Lee's. Upon the whole, it is a fair estimate that Lee's losses in killed during these operations did not exceed twenty-five hundred. Deduct this number, and we have 4,500 as the whole number of absentees who were lost to Lee from the beginning to the end of the operations, from any other cause than death, wounds or captivity. Of this number of absentees, as we have seen, fully 2,500 were lost to Lee at Five Forks and on the lines on April 2d, and never started on the retreat. The remainder, two thousand, dropped out of ranks between Amelia Court-House, where the great suffering for food began, and Appomattox Court-House. The number of all these absentees, under the adverse circumstances, would be far from proving that the army was melting away. As to most of these

*Grant lost 714 men at Battery Gregg.

absentees, their straggling or absence from their colors proves
rather weakness of body than waning fealty to their cause. The
fact that only two thousand of them succumbed to despair, famine,
or temptation to abandon their colors, on that long march to Appomattox, after nearly two weeks of continuous battle and terrible
suffering, affords sublime testimony to the heroic courage and fortitude of that other 34,000 fighting men who started on that
memorable retreat and none of whom were absent at the end,
save the killed, wounded and captured in battle.

GRANDEUR OF LEE.

In no part of his life did the grandeur of Lee shine more con-
spicuously than now. He was the same grave, calm Commander
in Chief; the same loveable tender man as in the days of power
and triumph. The troops who were wont to watch his counte-
nance to catch if possible an index of what was passing in his
mind saw nothing there which indicated despair. It was to this
bearing of their commander that in a large degree may be attrib-
uted the heroic efforts which the army of Northern Virginia
made, even to the last, to shake itself free from the toils of its
mighty pursuers. I well remember on the day after Sailors
creek, riding by some troops drawn up in line and momentarily
expecting to advance upon the enemy, who were discussing the
truth of the report that Ewell's corps had been captured there,
and how a private produced conviction of the falsity of the news
by indignantly asking: "Didn't you see Mars Bob when he rode
by just now? Did he look like Ewell's corps had been captured?"

At times on this retreat his bearing towards young officers
who came about him assumed a cheerfulness that almost
amounted to playfulness. To an officer sent by a Corps Commander to ask at what point Gen. Lee wished it to camp that
night, he replied, "Tell him to march them to the Virginia Line."
When the officer expressed surprise and asked how far it was, the
General pleasantly remarked, "Well then, tell him to march as
far as he can." On another occasion Gen. Lee was enquiring for a
place called the "Stone Chimneys" on his map, and was told by a
young officer who had been reared in the neighborhood that the
place where they then were must be the one marked upon the
map, for he remembered distinctly when the chimneys were built.

Gen. Lee, who evidently did not share the officer's confidence as to the locality, pleasantly remarked : " I was waiting for the guide to come up that we might ascertain from him, but I suppose we had as well go on. If you remember when the chimneys were built, this is not the place. The stone chimneys mentioned in this map were built before you were."

Near Farmville he sat for some time on his horse near a section of Chamberlayne's battery, which on the brow of the hill was shelling the enemy, and gazed intently through his glasses at their movements. He was quite exposed. Receiving a report from a staff officer, General Lee gave him a message in reply and as he started off said to him : "You rode up on the wrong side of the hill and unnecessarily exposed yourself. Why did you not come up on the other side ?" The officer said he was ashamed to shelter himself when his commander was so exposed. General Lee remarked to him quite sharply : "It is my duty to be here ; I must see. Your duty does not require you to see, or to expose yourself when there is no occasion for it. Ride back the way I tell you."

Near Goode's Bridge he astonished a young staff officer, after receiving a message sent by him, by looking quite fixedly at him and asking if "those people surprised your command this morning?" The officer was taken aback at the question, for he had just made a report from his commander that the troops were in good order, and asked directions for their disposition. He replied no, and asked if any such report had come to him. General Lee replied that he had received no such report, but that "judging from appearances something urgent must have prevented you young men about headquarters from making your toilets this morning," and he thought it possible that the command might have been surprised. At the same time he pointed to the officer's new cavalry boots, the leg of one being outside of the pants, while on the other the leather was half stuffed inside the pants, making that leg somewhat resemble a huge misshapen bologna-sausage. The young officer had not observed this until his attention was called to it, and his face turned blood-red at the rebuke, and he could not conceal his mortification as he saluted and started to return.

Gen. Lee then called him back and said he intended only to caution him as to the duty of officers, especially those who were near the persons of high commanders, to avoid anything on

a retreat which might look like demoralization : that he knew he
was a good soldier,and he must not take his caution so much to heart.
So self-contained and so considerate was this great man of the feelings of others that he paused in the trying moments, when the
destiny of a Nation and the fate of a retreating army were engross-
ing all his care, to soothe the wounded feelings of a young subal-
tern.

When one of the columns was some distance from Amelia
Springs, two men, young and handsome, well mounted and
dressed as Confederate officers, joined the troops, and rode some
distance with them. Their actions excited suspicion and they were
arrested and searched. On one of them was found a dispatch from
Sheridan to Grant. The two men then confessed that they were
scouts and spies for Sheridan.

A staff officer was directed to carry the dispatch to Gen'l. Lee,
and also to ask "what disposition to make of the spies," who now
momentarily expected to be led out to execution. Gen. Lee was
found late that night, at his head-quarters near Amelia Springs,
and the dispatch and message delivered. He enquired briefly of
the circumstances of the arrest of the two men, and whether any
information other than that sent him had been extracted from them.
Being answered, he turned to give instructions to some other officers, telling the staff officer to wait, he would give him his answer
presently. When he had finished giving his instructions to other
officers who were waiting, he again turned to the staff officer as if
about to speak to him, but remained silent for more than a minute
when he said, "Tell the general the lives of so many of our own
men are at stake that all my thoughts now must be given to dis-
posing of them. Let him keep the prisoners until he hears further from me." At the time it did not occur to the officer, though
it did shortly afterwards, when the surrender freed these spies of
their peril, that Gen'l. Lee was thinking, while he paused, that a
few hours would decide the fate of his army, and that if the army
were lost, the execution of the men would be useless. and debat-
ing in his own mind, whether, under the circumstances, duty for-
bade his showing pity for his captives, and giving them a chance
for their lives, by delaying a decision which. if made then, would.
according to all the laws of war. inevitably doom them to death.

REASONS FOR HOPING SUCCESS.

There are some who teach the children sprung from the loins of the Confederate soldier that it was folly to nurse the hope. that the men of 1861 could maintain their undertaking. Their convictions of honor and duty left them no alternative; but were it otherwise, can it be matter of reproach that they bared their own breasts to the storm rather than bequeath the battle to their children?

The falsity of the so called maxim, that "God favors the heaviest battallions" was signally illustrated by Napoleon throughout the greater part of his marvelous career. Charles XII of Sweden set it at naught. Frederick the Great won victory in spite of it, in the Seven Years War against nearly all Europe. Alexander, Hannibal and Cæsar in ancient days taught that numbers did not necessarily win battles.

The thought ignores Providence, and forgets the influences of moral forces in the work of war. All history sustains the profound philosopher, who declared that other maxim, "In war the moral is to the physical as three to one," and that maxim fights for the invaded against the invader.

The history of Western Europe did not allow the conclusion that it would respect the thin blockade which prevented the exchange of our great products in the markets of the world, and kept from us money, supplies and munitions which could not be had at home.

There was reasonable hope, if the contest long continued, that the interests and rivalries of the outside world would raise up allies for us, as in the Revolution of our fathers.*

*The Seizure of Mason and Slidell from an English vessel on the high seas' and the irritations and complications growing out of the French occupation of Mexico, came near involving the United States in conflict with those powers. The thin, almost "paper" blockades, maintained for a time on parts of the Southern coast, afforded constant provocations of trouble with the outside world, and so also of questions with foreign powers, which recognized the Confederate States as "belligerents," as to allowing our privateers to remain in their ports, the sale of ships, munitions of war, &c., &c , as where the Wachusetts attacked and cap. tured the privateer Florida in the Brazilian port of Bahia.

History taught that critical periods always arise in such a struggle, when military disaster or great sacrifice paralyze a representative government in carrying on a long war of invasion.*

---

*Such crises more than once threatened to bring invasion to a halt, during the last two years of the war.

In 1863 there was intense opposition to the draft and the methods of President Lincoln's administration both in the East and in the West. The terrible draft riots in New York city occurred while Meade was yet about Gettysburg. Had he been defeated there, the Government would have been compelled to call back its invading columns to enable it to maintain itself at home and save its capital. Such a result, a practical defensive, in the third year of the war, would have so greatly impaired, if not destroyed, the credit of the Government, and so strengthened the opposition at home, that it would have been impossible to fill the depleted armies, or successfully prosecute further invasion.

Another still more critical period arose in the latter part of the Summer of 1864. In the Spring of that year the Confederates had crushed an invading force in Florida, and practically ended the seige of Charleston. Banks had been defeated with great loss in his Red River campaign, and Sherman, after the defeat of his cavalry, compelled to fall back from his attempted invasion of Mississippi, and Hoke had captured Plymouth and expelled the enemy from North Carolina, while the Confederates had met with no corresponding back-sets.

Sherman had penetrated near Atlanta, but with considerable loss, and his ability to either capture the city or destroy Johnston's army was doubted, while few thought he could long maintain himself so far inland, and many believed he must finally retreat, which he could not do without great disaster. Grant had sustained fearful losses in the Wilderness, at Spottsylvania, at Cold Harbor, in assaults on Petersburg, and at the Mine explosion. The Confederates still holding Grant at arm's length before Richmond, had invaded Maryland and thrown an army up to the very walls of Washington, driven Hunter from Lynchburg, defeated Seigel in the Valley, and bottled up Butler at Bermuda Hundreds.

To popular conception of the North, the invading armies appeared at this time as far, if not farther, from accomplishing their task than in 1862, and there was great and almost universal despondency as to the final result of the war in the Northern mind. The depreciation of the currency was very great, and the strain of the war also added to the general feeling of despair. The Confederate cruisers had destroyed the United States merchant marine and practically driven it from the high seas. To cap it all came another of the interminable succession of drafts, demanding half a million more men to fill up the depleted armies, which still further fed public discontent and aroused most bitter opposition to further war of invasion.

Halleck, who was then Chief of Staff at Washington, writes Grant that alarming combinations were forming in several Northern States to resist the draft. He says: "The draft must be enforced, for otherwise the army can not be kept up, but to enforce it may require the withdrawal of a considerable number of troops from the field. I call your attention to it now that you may make your arrangements accordingly." "Are not appearances such that we 'ought to take in sail, and *prepare for a storm*'" Grant, on the 15th day of August, replies that the loyal governors must enforce the draft with their militia. "If we are to draw

Frederick the Great said that "an army, like a serpent, moves on its belly," and it was a rule of Cæsar's, in conducting invasions, that "war must support war." In a thinly settled country like ours, war could not be made to support war; since under such conditions "concentration starves itself." The offensive power of an army is gone at a long distance from its source of supply; and the necessity of maintaining long lines of communication often causes the retreat of the invader, though the invaded flees before him.

The character and expanse of country through which the invading armies must operate was, up to that time, a justification of the belief that the conquest of the South was impossible.

In the Revolution, England generally controlled the sea-board, but the river breezes were fitful and unsafe motive power for her sail vessels on our rivers, and she could not maintain depots of

troops from the field to keep the loyal States in harness, it will prove difficult to suppress the rebellion in the disloyal States. My withdrawal from the James *would ensure the defeat of Sherman.*" A week before Grant had written Sherman about reinforcing him, concurring in the latter's view "about showing no despondency" and expressing the opinion "we must win, *if not defeated at home.*" At that time, probably a majority of the voters at the North felt that war as a means of saving the Union was a failure, and the morale of the armies in the field were affected by the action of this opinion from their homes. Grant says, Memoirs, Vol. 2, p. 167, "anything that could have prolonged the war a year beyond the time it did finally close, would probably have exhausted the North to such an extent that they might then have abandoned the contest, and agreed to a separation."

All sources show that at this time there was great danger of a complete collapse of the war spirit of the North, and if the military successes at Atlanta and Winchester and Cedar Creek in September and October had not opportunely come to Mr. Lincoln's rescue just before the presidential election of November following, the "Peace Party" would have prevailed. Indeed, even after the fall of Atlanta, if Early, whose army had so nearly crushed Sheridan's on the 19th of October, had been able to finish the work, and to again invade Maryland and bring his army before Washington, it needs no seer to predict its effect on the Northern mind, or the change it would have produced in the presidential election. As it was over a million and a half of voters at the North expressed their dissatisfaction at the conduct of the war, and a desire in preference to save the Union by negotiations.

It admits of little doubt, if Sherman had been held off at Atlanta as Grant was at Richmond, and Early had been able to maintain his hold of the Valley, until after Nov. 6th, that the public opinion at the North would have destroyed the power of the government to continue a war of invasion. On such slender threads depend the fate of nations, and the chances of war give rise to many of them in a long contest such as ours was.

supplies for any large force, at any distance from the sea. It was not thought possible, under the art of war as known in 1861, that steam vessels could maintain inland navigation for any distance, in the face of modern shore batteries, or that railroads could be effectually operated through hostile country.

At last it was the power of the iron-clad steamer and the successful use of the railroad in maintaining long lines of communication—the first then unknown, and the latter then untested in war—combined with the control of the sea-board, which under Providence compassed our overthrow. Without the iron-clad steamer, Grant could not have brought or subsisted his army before Vicksburg. The historic ten months' seige which resulted in the fall of Richmond, would not have been written. The march to the sea and through the Carolinas could never have been undertaken, if a hostile navy had not controlled the coast. Without the railroad Sherman could not have reached Atlanta, nor Rosencrans have obtained a foot-hold at Chattanooga.

Who so impeaches the wisdom of our countrymen for engaging in unequal war, "may equally denounce Hancock and Adams and Washington and Jefferson, who declared the infant colonies independent States, and defiled the power of the greatest military government then on the globe."

THE PRIVATE SOLDIER OF THE A. N. V.

Who that looked on the private soldier of the Army of Northern Virginia can ever forget his bright face, his tattered jacket and crownless hat—his jests which tickled the very ribs of death—his weary marches in cold and heat and storm—his pangs of hunger, his parching fevers, his wounds—his passing away in woods or roadside when the weak body freed the dauntless soul—his bare feet tracking the rugged fields of Virginia and Maryland and Pennsylvania, some times with stains like those that reddened the snow at Valley Forge—his clinging to his colors while wife and child at home clutched at his courage with cries for bread—his hope and faith and patience to the end—his love of home—deference to woman and trust in God—his courage which sounded all the depths and shoals of misfortune, and for a time throttled fate itself—or the ringing yell of his onset, his battle anthem for native land, rising Heavenwards above the roar of an hundred stormy fields?

Who can forget his homeward march, after the end came, unstained by violence or wrong, and how the paroled prisoner became the citizen who won the admiration and wonder of the world? Let us emulate his example; and if misfortune or disaster bear us down, let us draw inspiration, as he did, from the sublime faith and fortitude of Lee, in the darkest hours of his life, and "trust to work out."

———

At the close of the address, Colonel Richard L. Maury offered the following resolution:

Resolved, That the thanks of this Association be tendered Governor Thomas G. Jones, of Alabama, for his able address on "The Last Days of the Army of Northern Virginia," and that a copy of same be requested for publication and the archives of the Association.

Adopted unanimously.

Major Thomas A. Brander moved that a committee of five be appointed to propose the names of the officers and the Executive Committee for the ensuing year. Adopted; and the following gentlemen were appointed: Thomas A. Brander, E. C. Minor, William Kean, Charles S. Morgan and A. W. Garber.

OTHER ADDRESSES.

In response to calls, Captain W. Gordon McCabe responded in a brief but beautiful address.

By this time the committee returned, and reported the names of the following gentlemen as officers for the ensuing year, and the report was unanimously agreed to:

President—Judge George L. Christian.
First Vice-President—Judge T. S. Garnett.
Second Vice-President—General Thomas L. Rosser.
Third Vice-President—Hon. R. T. Barton.
Secretary—Captain Thomas Ellett.
Treasurer—Private Robert J. Bosher.
Executive Committee—Colonel W. E. Cutshaw (chairman), Private J. T. Gray, Captain E. P. Reeve, Captain John Cussons, and Captain W. Gordon McCabe.

On motion, the meeting adjourned.

www.ingramcontent.com/pod-product-compliance
Lightning Source LLC
Chambersburg PA
CBHW030723110426
42739CB00030B/1358